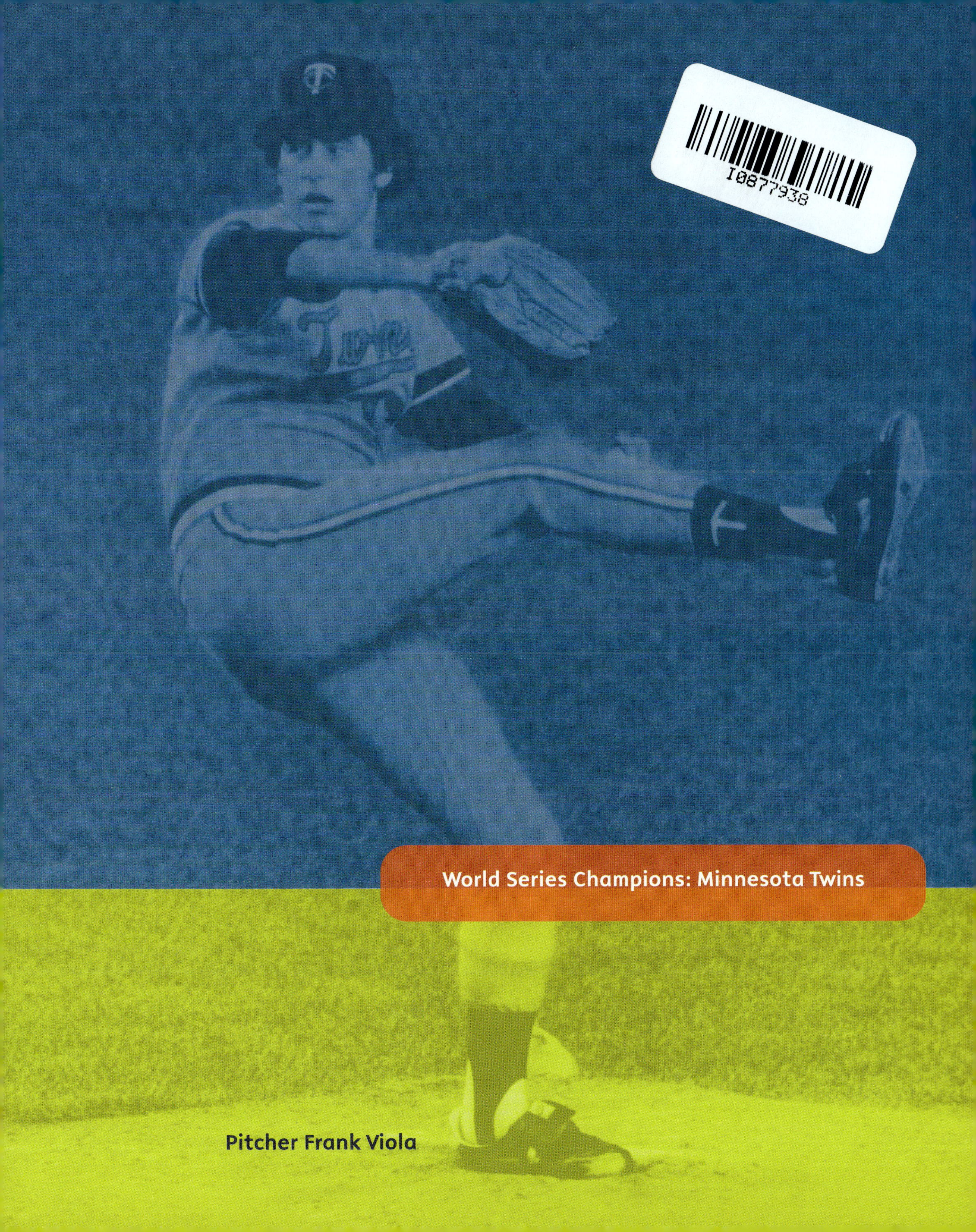

World Series Champions: Minnesota Twins

Pitcher Frank Viola

Shortstop Carlos Correa

WORLD SERIES CHAMPIONS

MINNESOTA TWINS

JOE TISCHLER

CREATIVE SPORTS

CREATIVE EDUCATION / CREATIVE PAPERBACKS

Published by Creative Education and Creative Paperbacks
P.O. Box 227, Mankato, Minnesota 56002
Creative Education and Creative Paperbacks are imprints of
The Creative Company
www.thecreativecompany.us

Art Direction by Tom Morgan
Book production by Ciara Beitlich
Edited by Jill Kalz

Photographs by Alamy (Cal Sport Media), Corbis (B Bennett, Hank Walker), Getty (Bettmann, Stephen Dunn, Focus on Sport, Brace Hemmelgarn, Bruce Kluckholm, Mitchell Layton, MLB Photos, Underwood Archives, John Williamson), iStock (f11photo)

Library of Congress Cataloging-in-Publication Data
Names: Tischler, Joe, author.
Title: Minnesota Twins / Joe Tischler.
Description: Mankato : Creative Education and Creative Paperbacks, 2024. | Series: Creative sports. World Series champions | Includes index. | Audience: Ages 7-10 | Audience: Grades 2-3 | Summary: "Elementary-level text and engaging sports photos highlight the Minnesota Twins' MLB World Series wins and losses, plus sensational players associated with the professional baseball team such as Joe Mauer."-- Provided by publisher.
Identifiers: LCCN 2023011761 (print) | LCCN 2023011762 (ebook) | ISBN 9781640268289 (library binding) | ISBN 9781682773789 (paperback) | ISBN 9781640009981 (pdf)
Subjects: LCSH: Minnesota Twins (Baseball team)--History--Juvenile literature. | World Series (Baseball)--History--Juvenile literature.
Classification: LCC GV875.M55 T58 2024 (print) | LCC GV875.M55 (ebook) | DDC 796.357/6409776579--dc23/eng/20230314
LC record available at https://lccn.loc.gov/2023011761
LC ebook record available at https://lccn.loc.gov/2023011762

Printed in China

1991 World Series Champions

Pitcher Bert Blyleven

CONTENTS

Home of the Twins

The state of Minnesota is well known for its many lakes. It has more than 10,000! Among all the lakes sits a **stadium** called Target Field. The Twins baseball team plays its home games there.

The Minnesota Twins are a Major League Baseball (MLB) team. They compete in the American League (AL) Central Division. Their **rivals** are the Chicago White Sox. All MLB teams want to win the World Series and become champions.

First baseman Harmon Killebrew

Naming the Twins

The club started in Washington, D.C. They were called the Senators. In 1961, the team moved to Minneapolis, Minnesota. The city is across the Mississippi River from the state capital of St. Paul. Together the cities are known as the "Twin Cities." The new team was called Twins.

Pitcher Walter Johnson

Twins History

The Senators began play in 1901. They were not very good. In 1904, they lost 113 games! They finally had their first winning record in 1912. Pitcher Walter Johnson won a lot of games. The Senators went on to win two AL **pennants** and beat the New York Giants in the 1924 World Series.

The Senators reached only one more World Series before moving in 1961. The team won almost immediately in Minnesota. Slugger Harmon Killebrew belted more than 500 home runs as a Twin. He led the team to the AL pennant in 1965. But they lost the World Series to the Los Angeles Dodgers.

The Twins returned to the World Series in 1987. Outfielder Kirby Puckett was a great hitter and fielder. He won six Silver Slugger and Gold Glove Awards. The best hitters and fielders win them. With his help, the Twins beat the St. Louis Cardinals in seven games. It was their first championship in Minnesota!

Outfielder Kirby Puckett

Pitcher Jack Morris

The Twins were back in the World Series in 1991. They faced the Atlanta Braves. Pitcher Jack Morris threw 10 **shutout** innings in Game 7. The Twins were champions again! Since then, they haven't returned to the World Series.

Other Twins Stars

Minnesota has had many stars. Joe Mauer was one of the best-hitting catchers of all time. He led the AL in batting average three times. Second baseman Rod Carew led the league in hitting for seven seasons as a Twin.

Johan Santana won two Cy Young Awards in the 2000s. The best pitchers win them. Frank Viola won the award in 1988. Bert Blyleven struck out a lot of batters.

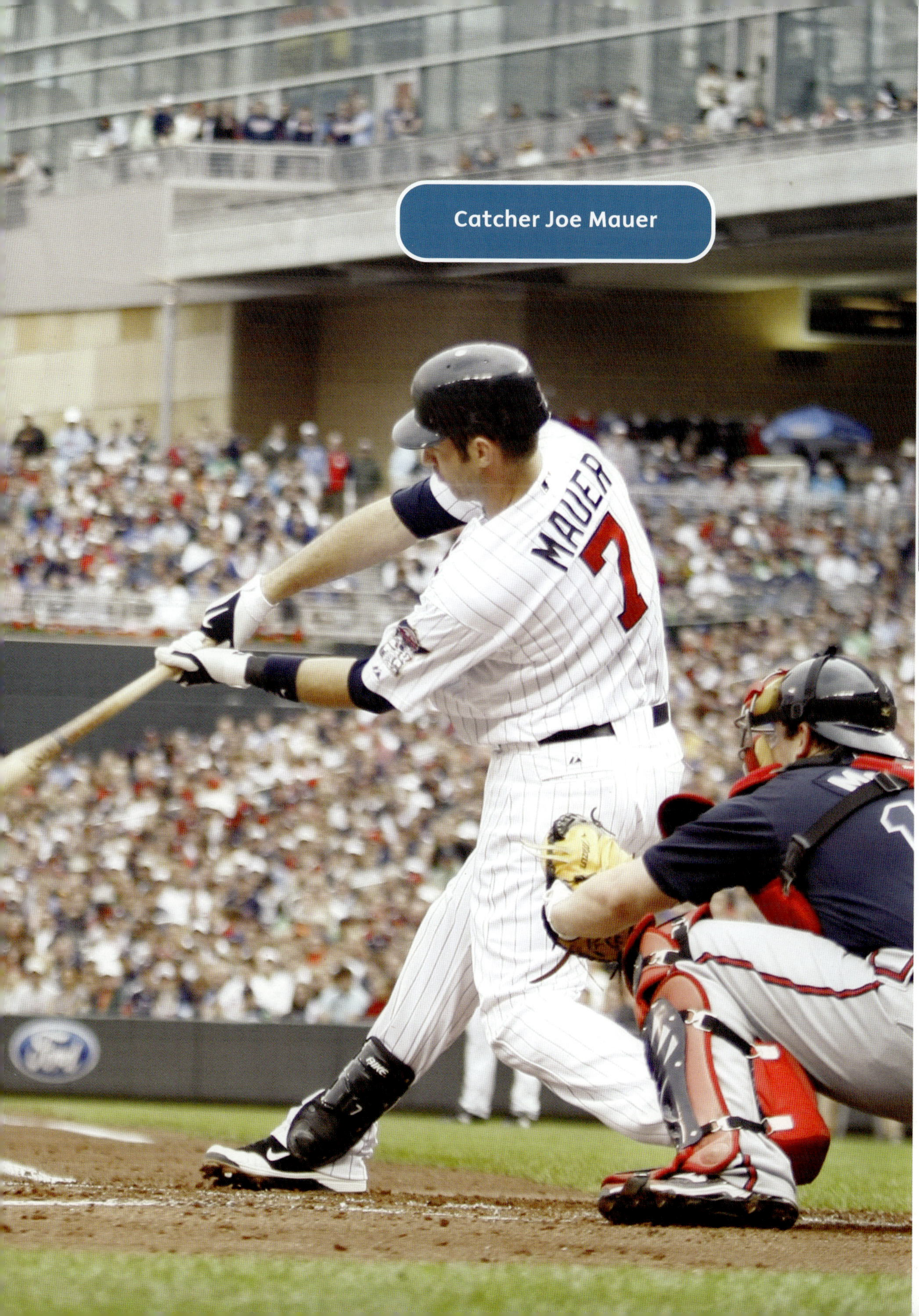

Catcher Joe Mauer

Outfielder Byron Buxton

Outfielder Byron Buxton is one of the best fielders in baseball today. So is shortstop Carlos Correa. Twins fans hope they can help bring a **title** to Target Field soon!

About the Twins

Started playing: 1901

League/division: American League, Central Division

Team colors: navy blue and red

Home stadium: Target Field

WORLD SERIES CHAMPIONSHIPS:

1924, 4 games to 3 over New York Giants

1987, 4 games to 3 over St. Louis Cardinals

1991, 4 games to 3 over Atlanta Braves

Minnesota Twins website: www.mlb.com/twins

Glossary

pennant—a league championship; a team that wins a pennant gets to play in the World Series

rival—a team that plays extra hard against another team

shutout—scoreless

stadium—a building with tiers of seats for spectators

title—another word for championship

WORLD SERIES CHAMPIONS

Pitcher Johan Santana

Index